Thirteen Steps
To Move From Victim Consciousness To God Consciousness

Healing From Traumatic Experiences, Including Sexual, Physical, Emotional, And Mental Abuse

Lawrence L. Doochin

Copyright © 2013 Lawrence L. Doochin
All rights reserved.

ISBN: 1481989987
ISBN 13: 9781481989985

Author's Note

Beginning around age twelve, I was sexually abused by my mother. Since this happened during the formative years of puberty, the abuse had tremendous ramifications as to how I saw myself and my concept of love, which became very distorted.

I came away from this experience with great anger, although I did not understand this at the time. I also came away with a large amount of grief, fear, guilt and shame around the experience, but I buried these in order to survive and continue operating in the world. During my twenties, I had a lot of anger at random situations or people, as this was really sideways anger from my abuse that was spilling out, like water boiling over the sides of a pot.

When I turned thirty, two things happened. First, I saw myself on an emotional healing path, as I started many years of intense therapy. Second, God awakened me to His Presence, and I saw myself moving onto a spiritual path. At the time I believed that I was on two separate paths, but these are really the same path, as God is Love, and we come back to Him through the emotions.

My thirties and into my early forties were a very difficult time for me and my family. I was doing intense work on healing the sexual abuse, and I had long periods where I was very depressed, angry, and fearful. These negative emotions poisoned my relationships with my wife and kids as I could not be the husband and father I wanted to be.

But at the same time, I knew that I could not stop midstream and that I needed to complete the process, regardless of the severity and length. I could only become whole by healing all of the grief, releasing all of the false beliefs such as guilt, which I had from the abuse.

I was given enough grace and short periods of joy and peace to know that there was a higher purpose for my experience and that I would not be in this hellish place forever. His Love carried me then and still carries me today, and for that I am very grateful.

Larry Doochin
December 2012

STEP ONE
Awareness and Recognition

In order to change something, you need only to be aware of the thing you want to change. It sounds easy and logical, right? But when we talk about patterns that someone has been accustomed to, it may not be so easy. When someone is used to doing something a certain way, even if that way brings them unhappiness, they may not be willing to change that pattern.

This is where awareness comes in. Are you completely happy with your life --- honesty is critical when you answer this question? If you are happy, then you can stop reading here. But if you would like to have more peace and joy in your life, maybe less anger, less judgment, then start with the simple recognition that your life is not working as you would like it to.

At this point, you don't have to know why. You just need to acknowledge that this is the case. If you have a relationship with God, this is where you ask for help. Even without a strong relationship with God, it is still beneficial to ask for help, to acknowledge that you cannot do it alone. Just voice it to God, your spouse, a good friend, or to no one in particular.

Asking for help is a type of surrender. It sends a message to yourself that you are not in control. You may think that you have been in control, and you may think that you can "fix" this problem on your own, but you have just acknowledged that your life is not working the way you want. That tells you that you have not done the best job of controlling things.

Acknowledging that you have not done the best job can be humbling for you, which is good, because humility creates the opening for surrender, change, and healing. The more someone tries to control their life, the more they resist and fear change. If you think of Life as a river, you can float effortlessly on the river, or you can try to control where you go by fighting the current. When you do the latter, you are bloodied and banged up as the current smashes you into the rocks.

So what is it that you need to become aware of? The simple answer is anything that does not serve you. How is this defined? This can be defined as anything that does not bring you joy **or** anything that blocks your natural joy. On the former you may purposefully put yourself into experiences that you know are not healthy for you. This could include addictions, toxic relationships, etc. These are actions or non actions (not removing yourself from a situation) you take which are harmful to your physical body, your emotional or mental well being, or your spirit. In terms of things that block your natural joy, false beliefs would fall into this category.

As children of God, we have His joy. That is our inheritance. You can feel that joy even in the midst of a dire situation. When we don't feel that joy, we are blocking it because of false beliefs that we hold. The problem with false beliefs is that they are not evident to us. They run underneath the surface like a computer virus.

Like a virus does to a computer, these beliefs affect the operation of you; they distort how you see yourself, others, the world, and God. The extent to which these distortions take place is the extent to which you hold false beliefs. Thus you see great degrees in how joyful people are as there are great degrees to which people hold false beliefs.

As you begin to recognize that you hold false beliefs that block your joy, you will also begin to take actions/non actions that put you into healthy situations that now bring you joy!

How do we recognize false beliefs so that we can change them? Recognize and be aware of the ways they get acted out. In what type of situations do you get angry and what are the triggers? What type of people do you not like to be around? What are the emotional patterns that you keep repeating?

In the subtitle of this booklet, I mention healing from sexual, physical, emotional, and mental abuse, but this really applies to any traumatic experience. Often in childhood, we have traumatic experiences that we may or may not remember. This is certainly true of young children who have been sexually abused. They often do not remember this experience.

Many children have also been either emotionally abused or neglected over a long period, which is very traumatic. As adults, they may remember that their parents were not loving, but they do not recognize how this affected them. Because children are developing in so many ways and must rely on their parents or caretakers for their very existence, traumatic experiences like abuse are very scarring. They can emotionally freeze a child at a certain age, dramatically altering the way that child sees themselves, from a healthy identity and sense of self to one where they believe that somehow they are not whole, not good enough. They have formed a system of false beliefs.

Children carry false beliefs into adulthood, and it alters everything in their life. Everything they do and say, their reactions, their relationships, are all viewed and formed through this particular lens of beliefs that is unique solely to them, because each of us has different experiences.

If a person can remember traumatic child experiences and can associate this with current adult triggers and situations, they have a big head start. But for many, they do not understand why they easily get angry at random things, why they cry or get fearful in certain situations. They do not understand why they cannot be more expressive of love to their spouse. They cannot understand or even recognize why they get a feeling of dread if they are around men with beards because as a child their abuser had a beard.

Childhood is almost always the source for unhealthy patterns that are repeated in adulthood, unless it is an experience like post traumatic stress disorder from war. When you experience repeat patterns, ask why and then unwind the false belief system back to that source. For instance, a woman who is in numerous relationships with abusive men can trace back her low self esteem to childhood because her dad showed little love. The good news, and the purpose of this booklet, is that everything false and unhealthy which was formed in childhood can be reversed, allowing someone to lead a very rich life filled with joy, peace, and God's Love.

STEP TWO
A Desire to Heal

Once you admit that your life is not going the way you want and there are certain patterns you want to change, you must desire that healing and change occur.

Many people resist this as they fear healing at a very deep level, whether recognized or not. They would rather stay with the known, even if that is fear, anger, dread, depression, or nonfunctioning relationships, versus going into the unknown. Recognition occurs that there is no turning back once one starts down the path of healing. It is like Alice going down the rabbit hole. This is your first test in faith and trusting in God that He has your highest good, that there was a higher purpose for your traumatic experience that you cannot currently see.

Healing can take many forms, and God loves us immensely. He individualizes the path and timing for each person, creating the most effective and gentle one based on that person's trauma, fears, desires, relationships and trust levels, and faith in Him.

At this point the path is unknown and that is good. Not only does the path change over time as God "reconfigures" based on your choices and progress, you would also fear the length or specifics of your healing if you knew what lay ahead. Also, certain understandings and changes are created only by going through an experience. You are able to release certain false beliefs not because someone told you that you held them, but because **you** experienced their falsity in some way.

It is not the experience itself that is the problem --- it is the fear of the experience, the belief it will be difficult, and the resistance to it which causes suffering. Just like in the river example, if you resist the natural flow, this makes it considerably more difficult. It will be as easy as you allow it. You may experience pain on the healing journey, but suffering is optional.

In addition, many people do not desire change as they want to stay in their victim persona or identity. These are the people who need attention. They are the ones who are always put out or complaining, who always tell people of their problems, who identify themselves as victims of something --- abuse, the world, other people, groups, nations, the government, situations --- the first time you meet them. Their belief is that they will find joy by acting this way. They can act very meek and appear to be frail, or they can be very opinionated and have a strong ego. In either situation, they feel that they need to do this to get noticed, and this is a false belief that comes from a distorted sense of self and worth. God and Oneness are empowering. Victimhood is disempowering.

Some people are in their victim persona all the time, as this is their primary identity, and many people move into it infrequently, as when they are trying to win an argument or trying to get something out of someone. Again, identification with victimhood goes back to the intensity of trauma that has occurred, usually creating a low self worth and negatively altered view of the world in more severe cases.

Additionally, there is a victim mentality that is collectively present in society and the world. This is reflected in the "us" versus "them" mentality, in the hatred of other individuals, groups, or nations. A victim, whether that is an individual, group, or nation, always has to have someone or something to blame. This is the opposite of God's Kingdom where there is no separation, no judgment or blame, only Oneness, true power, and Love.

The chapter heading is "a desire to heal." Once aware, you must have the desire to change what is not working. God doesn't need much, just a little willingness on your part --- He is pretty powerful and He can handle the rest!

If you recognize what you are doing and decide not to change it, that is certainly your choice. You have free will. It is important to recognize, though, that you are not getting what you *think* you are getting. You may *think* you are being safe; you may *think* you are controlling situations and people; you may *think* you are getting attention and joy when acting like a victim. What the ego mind *thinks* and what is true is vastly different. Your safety lies in God. You cannot control anything. And you cannot find any pleasure or joy in acting like a victim. You can only find *true* joy, peace, safety, and Love through healing, through God, and through a return to wholeness.

It is easy to stay where you have been, stay with what is comfortable for you, even if you live in a prison cell of your own making. But it takes a warrior and a lot of courage to break out of old patterns that no longer work, to jump into the unknown and know that God will catch you. Everyone fears and resists healing and change to some degree, so if you recognize that this is occurring, have great compassion on yourself. In doing so, you have already knocked off a big chunk of the healing process (more on this later).

STEP THREE
Allow the Process to Unfold, Including More Awareness

Now that you have made the decision to heal, what's next? Allow the process to unfold. What this means is allow God to take you down the path best suited for your healing. And be aware of everything around you, as the more aware you are, the quicker you can enter into the healing vehicles which He brings.

These healing vehicles or God hints can be an infinite number of sources --- the book that just happens to be left on a chair somewhere, the person who makes a random comment you overhear at the grocery, the animal that keeps appearing to you in person or in your dreams, how you get angry when the same circumstance or experience continues to "randomly" happen to you, the innocent comment your teenager makes that makes you feel guilty, the comment you hear about a great therapist or counselor who helped a friend of a friend.

Remember, there is nothing random in the body of God. He is One, which means that He is All, and you are part of that Oneness. Everything that happens to you has a purpose, even the most minor of encounters. The more you pay attention to this, the more you will see and understand the path of healing He has laid out for you.

You will also come to a much greater understanding of how much He loves you and how gentle, how non judgmental, that Love is. As part of this process, there may be times that you get angry with Him. This is normal and an important part of the unwinding of false beliefs. He welcomes this anger, because He welcomes anything that releases what is false in you and which brings you closer to Him.

Although you may temporarily move into anger and a victim identity related to God, it is critical not to stay there. God's actions or non actions are not to blame for where you are at. Many people will blame Him for what He is doing **to** them, or they will blame Him for what He is not doing **for** them. Do you see how someone might stay in the victim identity, blaming God in the same way they might blame a spouse for not giving them what they need in a relationship, a boss for not promoting them, a group for not accepting them, etc?

You are in a certain situation because of your choices that you have made. God is not punishing you nor denying you things you want. He is expressing through you (because we are One), and you are working with Him at a spirit level to create healing and wholeness within you. If you are seeing through only a worldly or ego perspective, you may not understand what is happening to you and you may see these things as negative. But that is because you are not seeing from a higher perspective (more on this in a later step).

Everything that is brought to you, without exception, is not random and is based on your will. God is just putting your choices into motion. If your ego tries to resist or detour where your spirit wants to go, this is when you see the manifestation of severe illnesses or tragedies that hopefully serve as a wake up call to what is going on within you at a much deeper level.

Again, God is very gentle. He wants the easiest path for us, but **we** are the ones who resist and make it difficult on ourselves. We forget that this world is not real and that what happens here is but a blip in eternity. We forget who we are in relation to Him, that we can never truly be harmed, never be hurt, never be separate from Him. Integrating pieces of a higher perspective into your healing process is a great blessing.

At this early stage of your healing process, recognize if you are in fear and trying to control the process. This is normal. Use that fear and need to control as a way to continually surrender to God. Acknowledge every day that you are in God's hands, that you do not know what is best for you, and ask that His Will be done for you.

Follow the hints that He gives you, because you are not only moving down the easiest path for healing but also learning to hear His voice instead of your own. A hint will be followed by an instant of knowing that this is His path for you. This is outside of your normal thought process. Trust this, even if it is only there for an instant.

Often your mind will attach to this idea and fear will set in. Many people come up with excuses, rationalizations, or just talk themselves out of following the hint, convincing themselves that this small opening of Heaven did not actually occur. Trust what He gives you, confirmed by your heart and gut, for this is Real. You will increasingly know what is best for you at a spirit level, what is meant by "to know thyself." This is Heaven opening up to you and an unfolding of great joy, peace, and Love. There may be future bumps in the road or small mountains to climb, but you have set yourself on a holy path.

STEP FOUR
Compassion, No Self Judgment, and Nurturing

This is actually a step that intertwines throughout every stage of the healing process and every part of your life. Having non judgment and great compassion on yourself are the two most important things you can do --- they are the healing process, regardless of the specific experience you are healing.

After a traumatic experience, especially one from childhood, there is great self judgment. A child cannot understand and process an experience like an adult. The questions that become ingrained in their psyche are like the following. Why did this happen to me? Why was I a bad girl or boy to deserve this? Why am I not lovable?

This creates a very distorted sense of self, especially if the child is not able to talk about what happened because the parents were the perpetrators or they do not have the emotional capacity to deal with an issue such as abuse (the child senses this). Children learn to survive and create coping mechanisms to deal with the "reality" that is present in their upbringing. Also, many children who have been sexually abused never speak up due to tremendous shame and guilt, even with loving parents. They believe they are at fault for what happened. Even a child of divorce can hold a strong set of beliefs that they are responsible for the divorce. All of these false beliefs and a distorted sense of self and worth get carried into adulthood where they affect everything.

When healing an issue that occurred in childhood or adulthood, there is a great tendency to be very hard on yourself, believing that you are not doing it right or fast enough. Some condemn themselves for resisting or delaying the path God has laid out for them, or for falling "off the path." There is no right or wrong way to heal. There is no timeframe that you have to hit. And everyone resists and falls off the path to a certain degree!

Be gentle with yourself. Again, the experience that you are healing is somewhat irrelevant. It is the compassion and gentleness on yourself that opens the door to make healing easier, enabling you to move through any pain with ease and grace, because self judgment is the first false belief that arose from your experience. When you stay in the compassion, you have already begun reversing a large chunk of the distorted sense of self worth that was created when the traumatic experience occurred.

A great thing happens as you stay in the compassion on yourself. Even if you are in the muck, you can have compassion others. All judgment is a projection of self judgment. What is "inside" is reflected and projected to what you see on the "outside," to how you see others and the world. So if you greatly self judge, believing that you are not a good person, you will see others in that same light and you will see the world as evil. If you know your Oneness with God and know that you are Love, you will see others as part of that Oneness, see the Love behind all appearances. So staying in compassion for yourself is critical to what happens in your life.

If you make decisions from a place of great compassion, on yourself and others, you will always be following God's guidance and the highest good for you, anyone involved in your decision, and the world. Being very judgmental and not compassionate of others is your attempt to punish another person or group, which again is a projection of wanting to punish yourself. Recognize this, pull that projection back in, and realize the self judgment present. Ask for God's help in healing that concurrent with healing the specific trauma you went through.

Nurturing yourself is also key. You have a reservoir within you that can be drained when you do difficult healing work, and you want to refill that reservoir with things that center you in Him. This could be prayer, long baths, yoga, etc. Our bodies are electromagnetic fields. As we are bombarded with disruptive electromagnetic frequencies from technology, we need to bring ourselves back to equilibrium and His frequency of Love. Being in nature and in the sun not only accomplishes this, but it also helps to quiet the chatter of the world so we can hear Him.

The greater you become entangled in the world and its happenings, the farther you move away from what is Real. You can be in the world but not of it. Reduce the time you listen to the news and surf the internet or check email. Listen to music instead of talk radio. Don't turn on your phone for part of a day. If for one week you abstain from technology and walk in the woods daily, your life will be transformed and you will be able to process your healing with much greater ease. Taking the time to nurture yourself is integral to having compassion on yourself.

STEP FIVE
Let the Emotions Flow, Let Them Out

God is Love, a noun. When He becomes manifest in this world through you, in all of your experiences, that Love becomes active, a verb. In order to fully know His Love, we must be able to express His Love, which means we must be emotionally open, emotionally authentic.

As an emotionally open person, you are able to express your emotions in a completely forthright and non threatening manner. You are honest with yourself and others. Seeing clearly any agendas and motives you hold, you do not use them as weapons in your relationships, nor do you place unconscious burdens or expectations on others. You express Love freely without fear of being vulnerable or of being hurt, always attentive to what a person is telling you. If you are angry, it is expressed in a controlled manner that does not demean or punish. You do not gossip about others, conducting all of your relationships with great respect and compassion for yourself and those you are dealing with. You do not shame or guilt anyone, and you practice the golden rule --- treat them as you would want to be treated.

Sounds great, doesn't it? You may say that it is also impossible --- even if you could do that, others do not. But when you are emotionally healthy and open, the games and agendas that others try to play on you have no effect. So how do you get to this place of authenticity? You are already there. It is your false beliefs that were created from traumatic experiences that cover up this recognition. The more traumatic the experience, the greater the false belief system and the wounding, and the less emotionally open you are.

Because we come from God and are One with Him, we are born very emotionally open. Those with no traumatic experiences and emotionally open and loving parents are generally emotionally open individuals who contribute great Love and Light in this world. But even without a storybook life such as this, you can heal from your past, experiencing a large amount of joy and helping the world. In fact, those who have healed very traumatic experiences often shine brightly with His Light and have a great capacity to change the world.

You must allow your emotions to freely flow through you as you heal from your traumatic experience. Don't allow your beliefs or society's rules, such as a woman believing she shouldn't get angry, or a man believing he shouldn't cry, to short circuit the expression of these emotions. "Shoulds" bind you and the freedom that is your birthright from God. Your emotions come up to be expressed and released. If you restrict that, they end up controlling you and how you interact in the world, severely limiting your joy.

It is false to believe you can bury your past and these emotions. Does cancer eventually show symptoms? These unresolved emotions are like anchors which weigh you down and prevent you from being "Light." Lightness is of God, your natural state.

Emotions around a childhood traumatic experience like abuse that are not processed developmentally freeze that person at that age. As an adult, these emotions are acted out at inappropriate times, as in getting angry at random things. This is literally your five year old or ten year old throwing a temper tantrum, reenacting the emotional stunting that happened when the traumatic experience occurred but was not allowed expression. If you try to repress your anger, it becomes depression.

The key is to go to the source. Allow the emotions to be expressed, revealing the false beliefs behind them. Getting angry all the time is a sign. You are not really getting angry at what appears to be the outside source. This is just a trigger, a reminder, of something much deeper, and it is a trail to follow. You may be anxious all of the time, or depressed, or not able to feel joy --- all of these are trails to follow. God intends for us to live a joy filled life, and if you are not, this is your prompt to start asking questions.

You cannot think your way to healing. Expressing emotions means being present in the body --- this is the temple where God resides. There is a time for asking questions, and there is a time for letting the emotions flow. Don't allow your questioning mind to block the flow of emotions. You can always process your healing experience after you have fully released .

Congratulations on a major healing step if you have stopped an addiction. Recognize that the traumatic experience and false beliefs that caused the addiction may still be there and the appropriate emotions must be released for you to fully heal. Sometimes a "negatively" viewed addiction (i.e. sex or drugs) may be replaced with a more "positively" viewed one (internet, obsessive exercising).

Do not judge the emotions that come up nor judge yourself. Stay in the moment, fully present with that emotion, allowing it to flow through you without resistance. When there is no judgment present, even if you are in the lowest valley, you can feel God's

Presence, supporting and lifting you. Try to have no expectations about how the healing process should look. Also, gratitude will carry you a long way, especially when you fall into self pity.

STEP SIX
The Manna

Anger and grief are emotions that are at the root of almost all traumatic experiences, and these are often accompanied by fear, shame, and guilt, especially if we are speaking of some type of abuse. Anger usually acts as the dam to a deep reservoir of grief. Let us distinguish between anger that is used as a defense against healing and anger that is related to the traumatic experience.

The former consists of those individuals who repeatedly use anger as part of their victim identity. The latter consists of anger that is coming up to be released. It may initially be sideways anger (not yet tracked back to its source), or it can be actual anger as part of the healing journey, like toward the abuser. Under either scenario, anger should not be a lifestyle. It acts only as a trigger and reminder or as the actual healing vehicle to get to other emotions such as grief.

When you experience random sideways anger, allow that anger to point you back to the true source of anger, like abuse. Express it so you can get to the grief and other emotions behind it. You are not continuing to heal if you stay angry at the perpetrator for an extended time. What is extended is unique to each person, but you will know if you are delaying further healing. Often people will stay in the anger to punish the perpetrator, but this only hurts you.

Does anger need to be expressed directly to the perpetrator? This again will be unique to each individual and will be a decision you make with God. Maybe that person has died. Maybe they are not in a mental state where they can understand what they did. What purpose does it serve?

Look at your motivation for wanting to stay angry and/or confront them (more on this in a later step), as this will teach you a lot about yourself. Sometimes expressing anger and confronting a perpetrator can have a huge healing effect for you as well as possibly the perpetrator, so there are no absolutes. As always, follow your God guidance in making these decisions. Do not make the decision when you are angry and controlled by your emotions.

In abuse situations, guilt, shame, and fear often accompany anger and grief. A child may have shame, especially if it is sexual abuse that felt physically good to them. They feel guilty as if they were responsible, as if they somehow invited it on themselves, and they feel fear around the incident. They feel fear in many forms --- physically for their life as that adult has great power over them, fear over it happening again, fear over someone finding out --- and this fear becomes ingrained in them, carried into adulthood and manifesting as anxiety, fear of being intimate and vulnerable in relationships, or just a general fear of death.

In addition to or in lieu of anger and grief, shame, guilt, and fear can be the triggers and reminders that healing is needed. Do you feel fearful or anxious a lot of the time? Do you easily feel guilty over things? Some of this may not relate back to abuse, but all of it is an indicator that something is amiss.

Shame, guilt, and fear are not of God. They are the products of a distorted mind, but they can be blessings to you if you allow them to lead you back to God and wholeness. Do not judge them, as self judgment only keeps you in a downward cycle. They are arising to help you heal, and if they make you very uncomfortable like a burr in a saddle, that is their purpose. Feeling uncomfortable creates a desire to change what is not working.

Anger, grief, fear, shame, and guilt --- none of these feel good, so we assign a "negative" connotation to them.

But they are manna from Heaven, because they are the reminders and vehicles to heal, bringing us back to Him. Remember, everything is of God. There are no absolutes except Him. Whether you assign something a "positive" or "negative" value is based on how **you** view it, which is based on **your** experiences and belief system **at that time**.

If you feel shame and guilt from sexual abuse or other traumatic childhood experiences, remember **that you were a child**. A child is at the mercy of others --- those who are supposed to love and be responsible for them. A child **is not responsible** for what the adult does to them or with them.

Responsibility lies with the adult, and they have abrogated that when they commit abuse. A child cannot say no to an adult without fear for their life. A child cannot help if they feel physical pleasure in the body when they are stimulated. Healing is possible if you have fear, shame, and guilt around what happened to you. As an adult, you can recognize how these were formed but that they no longer serve you. God's grace will help you to release shame and guilt. His Presence will **always** dissolve fear instantly. Ask for His help constantly.

For an abuse victim, after the dam of anger is breached, immense grief is present. This grief needs to be allowed expression. It may feel as if the grief will overpower you or never leave you, but this is false. It comes in waves as you spiral down to reach deeper levels.

Allow yourself to feel the grief fully, and trust in Him. How long does the grief last? The short answer is however long it takes to release it all. If you resist it or try to stop it, it will take longer. No one knows the timing, but know that God is there with you, experiencing what you experience, cradling you in His arms and His Love, making it as gentle a process as possible.

Comparison to and judgment of another's healing journey, even if it is your same issue, does not serve you in any way. Know that you never have enough information, you can never see the complete picture, in order to make an accurate assessment.

Self compassion, patience, staying in the moment, staying present with the grief, staying present in the body, are critical as you go through this process. Many people, having worked through numerous layers related to the abuse (anger, grief, guilt, etc), are exhausted and want an end to it, but let the process fully run its course. Great joy awaits you.

As previously discussed, we are meant to live life with the fullest joy. This is our natural state, our inheritance as a child of God. Grief blocks us from fully feeling that joy. We have been discussing individual grief related to traumatic experiences. And there is a collective grief that is present in the world, because we live in a dream of separation. We falsely believe, individually and collectively, that we are separate from God, which creates a great amount of grief and sadness at a level of spirit, manifesting throughout our whole being.

When healing grief from a traumatic experience, you will be tapping into the collective grief as well as your individual grief from your belief that you are separate from God. This is an opportunity to heal both, coming out with a recognition of your Oneness with Him, revealing the joy and peace filled person that is your true Self. This is not only possible; it is your destiny. You are here to make this journey back to Him, and all of your experiences, all of your relationships, "good" or "bad," have led you to a remembrance of this blessed journey.

STEP SEVEN
Reclaiming Parts of Yourself

A child who is abused is a survivor. They figure out how to continue to exist. That means that they "lose" parts of themselves. The "part" which has been abused is buried, because they are not in a safe and supportive place where they can feel the anger, grief, etc. at that time. Other "parts" step up and create a way, an identity, to continue living and operating in the world. Often this means a very dysfunctional identity and way of engaging with others if that person has been severely traumatized.

You don't really lose parts of yourself. You are whole. But you **believe** you are not whole, thus the need to heal this perceived schism.

As an adult, you can heal and reclaim the lost parts of yourself. You return to wholeness and a unified Self. The nurturing absent from your childhood is provided by the part of you living in unity with God, because He is the healer. He works through you and in Oneness with you to bring you back to your Self. Because we are One, everything longs to leave the dream of separation and return to unity, so all of your "parts" long to come home to complete themselves and return to wholeness. This is a very holy process of recreation that occurs within you.

STEP EIGHT
An Attitude of Gratitude

Gratitude is essential throughout the whole healing process and in life. When we recognize our Oneness with God and we feel His Presence, we are very grateful.

This gratitude extends to all areas of our life. Gratitude will always reverse the greatest self pity. It will raise you up from the lowest depression. If you are having a hard time being grateful, find one small thing to start with. This could simply be that you are alive, able to take a breath. If you are physically disabled, you still have a strong mind and the capacity to love, to know Him. You can be grateful for the sunshine, certainly for your children or spouse. There is a world of wonder, joy, and Love that awaits you, and God will help you find something which touches your heart and makes you grateful. When you find that first thing, you will find others.

Our attitude of gratitude must be practiced, because many have fallen into the habit, fallen into believing that it is normal, to live in self pity or with a darkened outlook of life. Practicing gratitude is especially important in the healing process --- if you are in the muck, it is easy to fall into self pity or anger. Gratitude will soften what you are experiencing and bring up the self compassion that is so important.

When you can laugh at yourself and your journey, laugh at your fears and your irrelevant thoughts, you are very grateful. Enjoy the laughter to the fullest degree as it is a support for your healing. When we laugh, God laughs, and we have **and** become His joy.

STEP NINE
OMG, Again?

As briefly mentioned earlier, there will be times when you have just had enough of the healing, both from length and severity as well as revisiting the same issue repeatedly.

For instance, grief over sexual abuse may be processed over a long period. The "down" periods between grief releases are as important as the grieving periods themselves, because in these consolidation periods your spirit and emotional body process the last round and prepare you for the next. God wants you to survive the process, and it's unlikely you can process all the grief in a short time. Be grateful for the joy and peace present in these consolidation periods. You will feel His Presence, and these breaks will refresh you, providing sustenance for the next round.

Different triggers will alert you to the next round of release, and follow these prompts, giving yourself the time and a place for this next healing. You are not doing anything wrong when the next one arises. You are exactly where you need to be, just a deeper level. It may not feel good and you may get angry, but your spirit has asked this of God. Being in a birth canal, the process cannot be stopped midway. Ask God's help for patience and for a higher perspective. Ask that the healing occur within you with the greatest ease and grace, and this will be done.

As I asked earlier, how long will you be in the healing process --- whatever is needed to become the joyful and Light filled person you were meant to be, one who fully knows God's Love. God's Grace is unlimited. Even if you don't feel it, it is shining upon you.

We are in a period where His Grace is accelerating healing for those who have committed to this process. Know that He is helping you to move as quickly as possible, as He longs for your return to Him. Learning patience is part of the journey. Stay in the moment versus being fixated on the future and a completion. When you stay in the moment, in the Now, you are truly in Unity with God, where all healing occurs faster, with great ease and grace.

STEP TEN
Expectations

Great peace, His peace, will come to you by dropping expectations. When we have no expectations, everything in life is a gift.

For the healing process, drop your expectations of form and timing, as well as expectations of others. You are whole and complete, because you are One with Him and all that is. You need do nothing to reach this except drop false beliefs which act as an impediment to you recognizing this truth.

When you have expectations of those close to you --- to do certain things or act a certain way, to say certain things

--- you are looking outside yourself for confirmation, operating in the victim identity we discussed earlier. You require no confirmation as God provides all of your needs, all of your identity. Expectations of others places an unconscious burden on them that they resent, creating friction that prevents freedom and authenticity in a relationship.

Expecting others to acknowledge anything related to the trauma you experienced or to "feel sorry" for you regarding your healing process does not help you and may delay your healing. Now, if they volunteer their compassion, what a gift and blessing that is.

God will provide some type of community healing support as this is vital.

This may just be one person --- your spouse, a good friend, a counselor --- or it may be a therapy support group, a church or synagogue community. Healing cannot happen in isolation. Individual and collective healing starts and finishes with the false belief we are separate from God and everything and everyone in His creation. As more people heal, we will recreate the community of the unity of God, completely changing the appearance of the world.

If you have contact or could have contact with the person who perpetrated the abuse or the trauma on you, you may desire an apology, or at least an acknowledgment of their act. If they are unavailable or dead, you may want an acknowledgment from another person, like your mother if it were your father who was the abuser. Wanting this is very normal. But what will it bring you? Will it help you to heal? Is this your only outlet for the anger? Do you want to punish? Does this person still have power over you if you need an apology or explanation?

What is your responsibility in all of this --- your response ability? Do you not want to respond in all situations from a fully emotionally healthy self? When you do this, you see from a much higher perspective, able to give fully of yourself **without** taking away from yourself because God is your endless source.

Your experience is finished and cannot be reversed. It is past, and you are living in this moment. The most compassionate thing for yourself is the decision to make. This will also be the most compassionate thing for everyone else, including the abuser or the protector of the abuser. Maybe you don't want that for them. This is a time for great self honesty and reflection. This is an important part of your healing process.

In the end, it **always** comes down to your peace and joy. Expecting an apology will not help you. What if you had no expectations but received an apology and the ability to discuss the experience with the abuser? How powerfully healing that would be for both of you and the world.

Expectations are inseparable from forgiveness, which is discussed in the next step.

STEP ELEVEN
Forgive AND Forget

The standard belief around forgiveness is forgiving but not forgetting. This is not true forgiveness. This is a **concept** of forgiveness which society and religions have told us is forgiveness but which entails anger being stuffed "because anger is not of God."

When you truly forgive, no memory remains --- emotional memory that is. You remember the incident, but it becomes just another experience seen and understood from a higher perspective of purpose for your life (see step thirteen). You cannot truly forgive until healed from the traumatic experience, and you have healed only after processing all of the emotions around it. This occurs when you think of the experience and it no longer brings up negativity.

To forgive but not forget does not set you free. You are still tied emotionally and energetically to the experience, and this concept of forgiveness can be an excuse or defense against actually healing the experience, never addressing the false beliefs that were created.

False forgiveness aligns with the false belief that God is a judgmental and punishing God who loves us but does not forget that we have sinned against Him. Thus the rationale to not forget when we forgive --- punishing the person as God still punishes us.

God is a God of Love. His Love is not like human love. His forgiveness is not like human forgiveness. God loves us beyond our comprehension and He sees past the errors we make to His holy child who is One with Him. He sees past the sinful self portrait we hold due to our false belief that we have separated from Him.

So to truly forgive the perpetrator of the abuse, or just someone you feel has wronged you, you see past their actions to the God within them. This is reality over illusion. True forgiveness comes from the heart, not from the head and your thoughts. This forgiveness is the basis of Divine Love. You will know with complete certainty when you have forgiven with God's Love. You will feel much lighter, very joyful and peaceful. You will feel free.

This is the capstone of your healing journey.

STEP TWELVE
Feelin the Healin

Through our Oneness with God, we create and manifest something into form by feeling the joy of its success **as if** it has already happened. The passage of time is an illusion that is part of the dream from which we are awakening. Only the present moment exists, and when we feel the joy as if it has already happened, we are birthing it in spirit, a prerequisite to that seed popping its head above ground. This is true of a project, the birth of a new company or a relationship, your healing process, etc.

What will it feel like when this traumatic experience no longer casts a shadow on you? Yes, this is not only possible --- it will happen. In God, all things are possible, and it is His Will that you heal and return to wholeness. So believe it, and feel it. Feel the joy, feel the peace, feel the relief as if you are free right now, free of the prison you have been living in. When you feel it, you have already become free!

STEP THIRTEEN
God Consciousness

God consciousness is not some grand concept available to just to Jesus and a select few. "In the world but not of it" is how you are meant to walk the world --- Jesus and many others have told us so. Nothing is required of you other than releasing what is false inside of you.

When you walk the world as an authentic and conscious human being, you don't play games or have agendas in your relationships. You interact with respect, honesty, directness, compassion, joy, and Love, and you see others as yourself, for we are One.

You are a magnifier of God's Light and Love versus being a dimmer switch.

God consciousness is a higher perspective. The perspective you have currently is not "wrong," but when you move to a higher step, you will see that you did not have all the information you needed to understand what you and others were experiencing. If your face is against a tree, you cannot know that you are in a forest. That requires moving to the top of the tree.

As part of the healing journey, a higher perspective enables you to stop resisting and to flow gently with your healing as you understand the higher purpose behind your traumatic experience. God always has our highest good. Regardless of the severity of the experience, He can make lemonade out of it if we allow Him. Good can come out of every experience, and every experience can help you remember Him and His Love.

If you are really blessed with a high perspective, you may see your experience as a gift. If the issue is abuse or another type of trauma, that perspective is often difficult for an outsider to understand, but the outsider is judging based on **their** experiences, beliefs, and values. These don't hold credibility as it relates to another's path. It is viewed as a gift because the healed person would not be at the level of God consciousness and understanding, would not have the peace, joy, and Love, without that experience having occurred.

This is very powerful, helping us to understand that everything truly is of God. There are no absolutes when it comes to "positive" or "negative" experiences. There is only "positive" and "negative" as it relates to how that person allows the experience to affect and serve them. Allow your lemon to be turned into lemonade with God's help.

Afterword

There is nothing I have written here that you do not already know. I am just helping you to remember.

God expresses through you, and you are One with Him, so you have all of the answers inside of you. Never look to another person, group, or organization for the Truth that lives in you.

His thoughts are love and peace based, confirmed in your heart and body. Your ego thoughts are fear based from a mind that constantly spins like a top. It takes practice to distinguish between the two, to learn to hear His voice in all situations. Ask for His guidance and Will for you in every moment. When you are uncertain, wait to make a decision, and keep asking. You will hear it. Trust that you have the answers, trust in Him, and you will always be fine.

God bless and much Love,

Larry

Lawrence Doochin is the author of "I am Therefore I am, Finding God in Our Heart," and "To Everything There is a Season, Sayings About Life, Love, and God."

He is also the creator of the very popular The Divine Speaks website (www.thedivinespeaks.com), which had over 80,000 visitors in 2012. When you go to the site, God will give you the "random" statement that is meant for you to hear at that time. There are almost 2000 statements on the site, and it is being used in many ways --- as a daily meditation or prayer, when someone is angry or going through a difficult time, when they have a question, or when they need help in seeing past a false belief. Lawrence posts a new daily statement on "Daily Light," which can be subscribed to by going to this website http://blog.thedivinespeaks.com/.

Finally, Lawrence is available for fee based spiritual and emotional counseling and can be contacted at lawrence@lawrencedoochin.com.

A digital version of this book is free and can be downloaded on The Divine Speaks website. This printed booklet is available for purchase only through Amazon.

Made in the USA
San Bernardino, CA
04 September 2013